P. J. CASEY

ROMAN COINAGE
IN BRITAIN

SHIRE ARCHAEOLOGY

Published by Shire Publications Ltd,
Midland House, West Way, Botley, Oxford OX2 0PH.
(www.shirebooks.co.uk)

First published 1980. Second edition 1984, reprinted 1988.
Third edition 1994, reprinted 1999, 2002 and 2009.
Transferred to digital print on demand 2011. Reprinted 2012.
Number 12 in the Shire Archaeology series
ISBN: 978 0 74780 634 9.

British Library Cataloguing in Publication Data:
Casey, P. J.
Roman Coinage in Britain. – 3Rev.ed.–
(Shire Archaeology Series; No.12)
I. Title II. Series 737.4937
ISBN-10 0 7478 0231 9
ISBN-13 978 0 74780 231 0

Series Editor: James Dyer

*Cover: Coin of the Emperor Claudius (AD 43-54).
(Photograph courtesy of the British Museum)*

Printed by PrintOnDemand-Worldwide.com, Peterborough, UK.

Contents

4

List of Illustrations

The coins illustrated in plates 1-15 are all reproduced actual size.

Preface

This book is not a key to the identification of coins found in the context of Roman sites in Britain; rather it is an attempt to place the coins in an historical and economic framework which defines the limits of inference within which coins may be used both as dating and as economic evidence. Individual sites may produce patterns of coinage at variance with those used as illustrations in this work. Such sites will be those which did not experience the full chronological life of the cited examples, since the events operating on the Roman currency usually took some time for their full effects to be felt and for these effects to be registered in the archaeological record.

Two important classes of site have been excluded from this study, villas and temples. Villa sites rarely produce very large numbers of coins simply because it was in the town that the farmer most often used money rather than on the estate. Temples, on the other hand, sometimes produce very large numbers of coins, but of a somewhat peculiar nature. Often the deposits consist almost exclusively of copies or of coins not normally found on urban or domestic sites. The incidence of inferior coinage can be explained by its comprising votive offerings which represented the spirit of giving rather than its substance. The unusual representation of coins from periods when they are otherwise scarce in archaeological deposits is due to their having been consecrated by virtue of their votive status. Such coins were not recirculated and thus did not re-enter the currency pool to be withdrawn by normal economic usage. In general value judgements have been avoided. Little enough is known about the economy of Roman Britain and deductions based on the incidence of extremely low-value coins are likely to be ill founded. Similarly no attempt has been made to equate the incidence of hoards with political or military events which are not attested by ancient sources.

It is a pleasure to record my thanks to C. C. Haselgrove for having read the script and made helpful comment upon it and to T. Middlemas for constant assistance in the field of photography. Messrs A. H. Baldwin proved a haven of scholarship, as they have over many years to many numismatists. Finally my thanks go to Dr J. P. C. Kent, whose years of teaching, both formal and informal, have stimulated my interest in Romano-British numismatic problems.

Department of Archaeology, Durham University.

1

The Roman imperial currency system

Although coinage had been in use for some years before the Claudian invasion, the full integration of Britain into the Roman Empire linked it with a society in which a state-backed currency allowed for the easy transaction of day-to-day business and for the accumulation and transport of wealth in a new way. The economic liberation of enterprise should not be underestimated: coinage permitted the transfer of funds to Britain through moneylenders to pay for the luxuries of Romanisation and the acquisition of property by non-Britons. The manner by which coinage reached the population is obscure, but the standing army of about thirty thousand men was probably the key to the matter. By the middle of the second century such an army would have been paid annually at least 6,750,000 *denarii,* and in practice perhaps one third or half as much again as this minimum estimate. A great deal of this money would be redistributed into the civilian economy, either by compulsory deductions made for provisions, the most important element of which, corn, was purchased by the Roman administration from native producers at a fixed price, or by individual purchases of equipment, clothing, extra rations and the other commodities which traditionally ameliorate the rigours of military life. To supply these needs, civilian communities attached themselves to military sites. Outside the military zone towns and cities sprang up under the encouragement of Roman administrative practices.

Plate 1. DENOMINATIONS: FIRST AND SECOND CENTURIES
1. Hadrian (117-38). *Aureus. HADRIANVS AVGVSTVS — COS III.* RIC 186 (125-8).
2. Tiberius (14-37). Gold *quinarius. T DIVI F AVGVSTVS — TR POT XXV.* RIC 4 (24).
3. Trajan (98-117). *Denarius. IMP TRAIANO AVG GER DAC PM TR P — COS V PP SPQR OPTIMO PRINC.* RIC 28 (103-11).
4. Commodus (181-92). Silver *quinarius. M COMMODVS AVG — TR P VIII IMP VI COS IIII PP.* RIC 68a (183-4).
5. Trajan (98-117). *Sestertius. IMP CAE NERVAE TRAIANO AVG GER DAC PM TR P COS V PP — SPQR OPTIMO PRINCIPI — SC.* RIC 543 (103-11).
6. Marcus Aurelius (161-81). *Dupondius. M AVREL ANTONINVS AVG TR P XXXIII — IMP X COS III PP — SC.* RIC 1241 (179).
7. Antoninus Pius (138-61). *As. ANTONINVS AVG PIVS PP — TR POT COS III — SC.* RIC 669 (140-4).
8. Nero (54-68). *Semis. NERO CAES AVG IMP — CER QVINQ ROM CO — SC.* RIC 378 (65).
9. Nero. *Quadrans. NERO CLAV CAE AVG GER — PM TR P IMP PP — SC.* RIC 414. (64-8).

Urban development and its concomitant entrepreneurial activity and manufacturing demanded a cash economy.

The currrency system brought to Britain by the Claudian conquest was that established by Augustus in 24 BC. The system was based on four metals: gold, silver, *orichalcum* (brass) and copper (plate 1 nos. 1-9).

Monetary relationships (first to third centuries)

aureus (gold)	*denarius* (silver)	*sestertius* (brass)	*dupondius* (brass)	*as* (copper)	*semis* (brass)	*quadrans* (copper)
1	25	100	200	400	800	1600
	1	4	8	16	32	64
		1	2	4	8	16
			1	2	4	8
				1	2	4
					1	2

There were also occasional issues of half *aureus* and half *denarius* pieces, called *quinarii* (plate 1 nos. 2, 4).

From time to time the weight and fineness of individual denominations were adjusted, almost invariably downwards, under the influence of economic pressures. The greatest fluctuation was in the weight and fineness of the *denarius*, which suffered a systematic decline under the pressure of increasing military expenditure in the second and third centuries (fig. 2). Base-metal issues tended to be reduced in weight to match the metallic decline in the *denarius*. The *aureus* declined in weight (from 7.75 grams in the mid first century to 2.45 grams in *c* 268), though not in fineness, in an attempt to retain the traditional relationship between denominations but, from the mid second century, gold coins probably circulated at a premium just as the sovereign now does, though not at anything like the modern disparate rate (fig. 2). As the intrinsic value of the previous metal coinage declined so its circulation volume increased — a well recognised symptom of an inflationary economic system — and the use of small-value copper coins diminished. Gradually the state shifted from producing a large volume of *asses* and a small proportion of higher-value denominations to issuing relatively few fractions of the *sestertius*. In the later second and third centuries even the issue of *sestertii* was restricted in some provinces, including Britain, and shortly after the middle of the third century ceased altogether throughout the Empire.

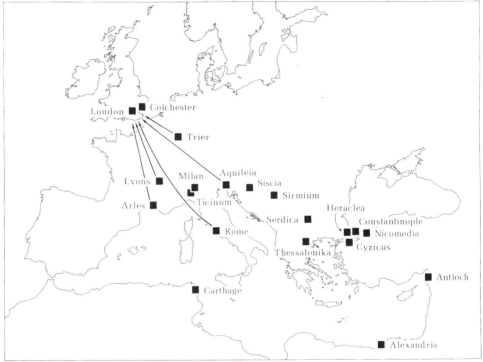

Fig. 1. Principal mints of the Roman Empire. Mints contributing to the coinage of Britain on a significant scale are indicated.

A fundamental change in the denominational structure was made by the emperor Caracalla in 215 with the introduction of a new silver coin, which is generally agreed to be a double *denarius*. This new coin was differentiated from the *denarius* by the treatment of the imperial image, which bears a radiate crown instead of the traditional laurel wreath (plate 2 no. 1). A similar crown had differentiated the *dupondius* from its half *as* since the reign of Nero. In reality what appears to be a crown did not exist as a piece of imperial regalia but represents the horizontal light rays which surrounded the head of Apollo, a deity particularly dear to the artistically gifted Nero. Despite its proclaimed notional value, the new coin, issued in conjunction with a number of other money-raising schemes, contained twenty-five per cent less silver than two individual contemporary *denarii*. The profit to the imperial exchequer, if it could make payments in the new coin, conventionally known as the *antoninianus* (i.e. [the coin of] Antoninus=Caracalla), and receive payments in *denarii*, would be considerable. The result was to drive *denarii* out of the currency system. This

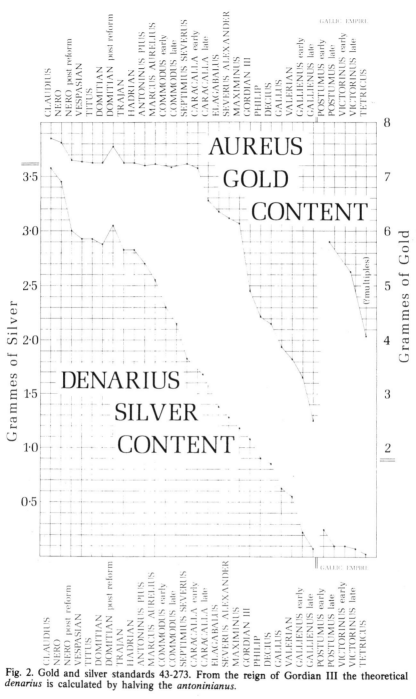

Fig. 2. Gold and silver standards 43-273. From the reign of Gordian III the theoretical *denarius* is calculated by halving the *antoninianus*.

did not take place at once; the *antoninianus* ceased to be issued between 222 and 238, then resumed its place in the currency and thereafter eroded the position of the *denarius* in the monetary system. By 244, the *denarius* ceased to be issued as a regular part of the currency.

From its inception the *antoninianus* was a debasement of the currency by a hard-pressed government. With the resumption of its issue the *antoninianus* suffered the same fate as had the *denarius* hitherto, being subjected to a series of debasements which affected both the weight of the coin and its silver content.

The reasons for these changes are not difficult to define. Throughout the third century the military threat to the Empire's frontiers, first experienced in the second half of the second century, grew in gravity and called for greater and greater expenditure on military operations. Frontier armies owing allegiance to their own provinces, in which they had been stationed for generations, elevated their own generals to imperial status. Between the death of Caracalla in 218 and the accession of Diocletian in 284 no less than thirty-seven emperors held imperial office as legitimate rulers or held usurped power in a province or group of provinces. Each of these rulers was constrained not merely to pay for a high level of military activity but to pay an accession donative to each of his supporters. The decline in the intrinsic value of the currency was dramatic; by the reign of Trajan Decius (249-51) (plate 2 no. 2) *antoniniani* were being overstruck on the few surviving *denarii*. In the following two decades the decline in the *antoninianus* accelerated until, in the reign of Claudius II Gothicus (268-70) (plate 2 no. 3), it had been reduced to a weight of about 2.5 to 3 grams, containing only two per cent of silver.

The effect of the collapse of the silver currency, the economic backbone of the system, had its repercussions among the other denominations. An attempt by Postumus (258-68) to revive the old imperial system of the *sestertius* (plate 2 no. 4) and its fractions, together with a radiate double *sestertius* (plate 2 no. 5), failed, and such denominations ceased to be struck except for exceptionally rare ceremonial issues. Clearly the intrinsic value of a *sestertius* was greater than that of the base *antoninianus* to which it stood in a relationship of eight to one, and its production was uneconomic. The inconvenience of the *sestertius* as an element of an economic system marked by grave inflation is emphasised by the fact that an *antoninianus* of 3.5 grams would have acquired about 200 grams of brass in an exchange in *sestertii*.

While the last stages in the demise of the Augustan currency system were taking place, the Empire itself had been riven by civil wars which resulted in its division into three major areas. The western provinces of Britain, Germany and Gaul created their own rulers from 258 to 273, the East fell under the control of the desert city of Palmyra and the Central Empire controlled Africa, Spain, Italy and the Balkans. The pressure on the monetary system operated equally on each of these rival regimes.

In 273 the Empire was once again reunited under the soldier-emperor Aurelian (270-5), who initiated a reform of the by now utterly discredited currency. Aurelian's reform is the subject of controversy but appears to have attempted to produce a billon coin of guaranteed weight and silver content. This new coinage, whilst intrinsically of no greater value than *antoniniani* of the penultimate standard of the Gallic Empire, seems to have been tariffed at an artificially high rate. Many of the new coins bore a mark of value XXI (or the Greek equivalent KA) which has been interpreted as indicating the intrinsic value of the new coins in terms of silver to copper content. The tariffed value of the coin was probably four *denarii* (plate 2 no. 6). A fractional coinage was also issued, a billon laureate (?) 2 *denarius* piece (plate 2 no. 7) and copper coins, in two modules, which may represent *sestertii* and *dupondii* (plate 2 no. 8) All fractional issues are of such rarity as to suggest that the coin reform in reality extended little beyond the XXI billon issue. Gold coinage was issued at a variety of standards; its relationship to the reformed currency is uncertain.

Aurelian's reformed coinage remained the standard for the reunited Empire until the reign of Diocletian. By that date the inevitable inflationary pressures had operated and, in 294 or 296, Diocletian completed a thorough revision of the imperial currency system as part of a comprehensive reform of all aspects of the government and administration of the Empire.

Plate 2. DENOMINATIONS: THIRD CENTURY
1. Caracalla (198-217). *Antoninianus. ANTONINVS PIVS AVG GERM — PM TR P XX COS IIII PP.* RIC 285(d) (217).
2. Trajan Decius (249-51). *Antoninianus. IMP C M Q TRAIANVS DECIVS AVG.*
3. Claudius II (268-70). *Antoninianus. IMP C CLAVDIVS AVG — IOVI VICTORI.* RIC 54.
4. Postumus (259-68). *Sestertius. IMP C POSTVMVS PIVS F AVG — PM TR P COS II — SC.* RIC 109.
5. Postumus. Double *sestertius. IMP C M CASS LAT POSTVMVS PF AVG — PM TR P COS II PP — SC.* RIC 106.
6. Aurelian (270-5). '*Antoninianus*'. *IMP C AVRELIANVS AVG — ORIENS AVG.* RIC 278.
7. Aurelian. '*Denarius*'. *IMP AVRELIANVS AVG — VICTORIA AVG.* RIC 73.
8. Aurelian. '*Dupondius/As*'. *IMP AVRELIANVS AVG — CONCORDIA AVGG.* RIC 80.

Diocletian's reform is the subject of much academic dispute. Unfortunately we do not yet have sufficient information even to place the coins into a framework of relative values with complete confidence. Nonetheless, newly discovered inscriptions and the scientific analysis of the metallurgy of the coins themselves allow a scheme of values to be proposed. A complication of this coinage arises from the continued use in ancient sources of the traditional names for sums expressed in accounts or price lists — *denarii, sestertii,* etc — which we cannot relate to actual coins. Yet another complication arises from the practice of revaluing coins by administrative edict without changing the physical composition or types of the coins themselves in any way. Such a change overtook the coinage in 301 when an edict was promulgated which tried, unsuccessfully, to establish the maximum market price for a wide range of basic commodities and services. In conjunction with this a revaluation of the coinage took place.

In *c* 286 as a preliminary to his reform Diocletian standardised the bulk of the gold coinage to a weight standard of one sixtieth of a Roman pound (5.4 grams) (plate 3 no. 1). The next step (*c* 293) was the resumption of the issue of a high-quality silver coinage at one ninety-sixth of a pound standard (*c* 3.4 grams), this coin being conventionally known as the *argenteus* (plate 3 no. 2). In 294/6 the billon coinage was reformed. The XXI radiate of Aurelian's reform was phased out and replaced by a new laureate issue of about 10 grams in weight and about 3 per cent silver content (plate 3 no. 3). Without ancient warrant this coin is generally called the *follis*. This coin was issued uniformly from mints established in

Plate 3. DIOCLETIAN'S REFORMED COINAGE
1. Diocletian (284-305). *Aureus.* DIOCLETIANVS AVGVSTVS — XX DIOCLETIANI AVG. RIC VI (Aquileia) 12 (303).
2. Diocletian. *Argenteus.* DIOCLETIANVS AVG — VIRTVS MILITVM. RIC VI (Siscia) 32a (294).
3. Diocletian. 'Follis'. IMP DIOCLETIANVS PF AVG — GENIO POPVLI ROMANI. RIC VI (London) 6a (*c* 300).
4. Diocletian. 'Denarius'. IMP DIOCLETIANVS AVG — IOVI CONSERVAT AVGG. RIC 193.
5. Constantine I (307-37). 'Follis'. CONSTANTINVS FIL AVGG — GENIO CAESARIS. RIC VI (Thessalonika) 32b (308-10).
6. Maximinus Daza (309-13). 'Follis'. IMP MAXIMINVS PF AVG — GENIO POP ROM. RIC VI (Trier) 845a (310-13).
7. Licinius (308-24). 'Follis'. IMP LICINIVS PF AVG — GENIO POP ROM. RIC VII (London) 3 (313-14).
8. Constantine I. *Solidus.* CONSTANTINVS PF AVG — SECVRITAS REIPVBLICAE. RIC VII (Trier) 502 (326-7).
9. Licinius. *Aureus.* LICINIVS AVGVSTVS — IOVI CONS LICINI AVG. RIC VII (Nicomedia) 18 var. (317-18).

1

2

3

4

5

6

7

8

9

nearly all of the *dioceses* into which, under new administrative arrangements, the Empire had been divided. With this aspect of the reform came the practice of systematically indicating the source of the coinage by placing a mint mark on the coins, a control device which had hitherto been only intermittently used. Two further denominations completed the reform, a small laureate issue in copper (about 1.3 grams) (plate 3 no. 4) and a copper radiate (about 3 grams).

An inscription found at Aphrodisias in Caria (modern southern Turkey) indicates that, whatever value the new coinage bore when it was issued, some, at least, of it was to be retariffed with effect from 1st September 301. The silver coin, the *argenteus,* was tariffed at one hundred *denarii* and some other denominations were to be doubled in value. If we assume that the hundred *denarius argenteus* was similarly valued before the retariffing, a scheme of denominations can be postulated which relates back to the original system as established by Diocletian's reform. It must be emphasised that this scheme is highly speculative and allows for a 25 per cent overvaluation of the copper coinage, against gold, by the issuing authority.

Diocletian's reform: the system before 301

aureus	argenteus	'follis'	XXI pre-reform	post-reform radiate	laureate copper (denarius)
1	15	150	?	750	1500
	1	10	?	50	100
		1	?	5	10
			1	?	?
				1	2
					1

Less speculative is the system pertaining after 301.

Diocletian's reform: the system after 301   (after Cope)

aureus	argenteus	'follis'	XXI pre-reform	post-reform radiate	laureate copper (denarius)
1	15	75	375	750	1500
	1	5	25	50	100
		1	4	10	20
			1	2	4
				1	2
					1

These values are based on minimum estimates derived from an analysis of the precious-metal content of the higher-value coins and relating these to the actual value of the metal in the coins as given in the contemporary 'Edict of Maximum Prices'. There is no evidence to judge by what factor the state over-valued any, or all, of its coins. It is normal practice for a coin-issuing authority to impose such over-valuation.

For a decade the Diocletianic reform held its own against economic pressures but, shortly after the abdication of the joint emperors Diocletian and Maximian in 305, a series of reductions in the weight of the laureate billon 20 *denarius (follis)* coin took place (plate 3 nos. 5-7). As this denomination fell in weight, the issue of fractions ceased with a few exceptions; *argentei* were discontinued after 308. At the same time the value of gold rose from 72,000 *denarii* per pound in 301 to 100,000 *denarii* per pound in *c* 309. The relationship between gold and silver coins and those of billon and copper became a fluctuating one reacting, on a day-to-day basis, to market forces. Political fragmentation led to the establishment of a number of conflicting coinage standards within the Empire. All, however, paid lip service to the Diocletianic scheme and the integrity of the gold coinage, as restored by Diocletian, was respected until the advent of Constantine the Great.

The career of Constantine and his progress from pretender based in Britain and Gaul to supreme ruler of the Roman world is reflected in the coinage, with Constantine's own currency system eventually prevailing over those of his various rivals.

Constantine had to overcome the problem that he held the least profitable areas of the Empire. To remedy this fiscal defect, in about 310 he reduced the weight of the gold coinage from the one sixtieth standard to one of one seventy-second (4.45 grams). This new gold coin, the *solidus*, became the standard high denomination of the Roman world with the elimination of Constantine's last rival, Licinius, in 324 (plate 3 nos. 8-9). Thereafter its integrity was jealously protected until the eleventh century. A high volume of output of gold, helped in part by Constantine's sequestration of treasure stored in pagan temples throughout his Empire, ensured that the *solidus* became the normal coin for use in large transactions.

Constantine's billon coinage initially followed the Diocletianic system and types down to the issue of a series bearing the legend *SOLI IN-VICTO COMITI* (To the unconquered Sun [my] companion), but in *c* 318 it diverged from the *'follis'* with the issue of even baser coins derived ultimately from silver prototypes issued from Trier in Constantine's early days of power (plate 4 no. 1). This new coinage, weighing 3.0 grams, with the reverse type *VICTORIAE LAETAE PRINC PERP* (The joyful victories of our everlasting ruler), appears to have been tariffed as a 12½ *denarius* piece (plate 4 no. 2). Surviving reduced *'folles'* of a higher intrinsic value rapidly went out of circulation. There is reason to think that this new coin was called the *centenionalis*, the name deriving from the fact that the base silver coin from which it had developed had originally been tariffed at the rate of one hundred to the *solidus*. Between 318 and 348, the date of the next important reform of the billon coinage, the *centenionalis* declined in weight from an initial 3.0 grams to 1.7 grams (plate 4 nos. 3-10). To supplement this coinage the issue of high-quality silver was resumed in *c* 325 at two standards, one ninety-sixth and one seventy-second of a pound. These coins are conventionally known, without the warrant of antiquity, as the *siliqua* and the *miliarense*. Silver continued to be issued in quantity throughout the fourth century, usually in association with donatives to the army, who received on the accession of an emperor a bounty of five *solidi* and a pound of silver, either in bar or coin. Minor imperial festivals, consulships, birthdays and such like all called for bounties at lesser rates than that paid for an accession. A number of silver standards prevailed, several at the same time or in different areas of the Empire. Nomenclature, as has been observed, is uncertain. See page 20.

With the establishment of a high-quality gold coinage and a regularly produced silver coinage, albeit at erratic standards, the currency needs of the upper levels of economic activity were well catered for throughout the fourth century. The collection of taxes, which this stable system was designed to facilitate, reverted to cash levies from the system of payment in kind which had been instituted during the monetary chaos of the third century. Nonetheless, the billon coinage still presented problems. In 348,

Plate 4. CONSTANTINIAN COINAGE, *c* 313-41
1. Constantine I (307-37). *Argenteus. IMP CONSTANTINVS AVG — VICTORIAE LAETAE PRINC PERP.* C 638 (313).
2. Constantine I. *Centenionalis. IMP CONSTANTINVS AG — VICTORIAE LAETAE PRINC PERP.* RIC VII (Trier) 208a (318-19).
3. Constantine I. *Centenionalis. CONSTANTINVS AVG — VIRTVS EXERCIT.* RIC VII (London) 185 (320).
4. Constantine I. *Centenionalis. CONSTANTINVS AVG — BEATA TRANQVILLITAS.* RIC VII (Lyons) 130 (321).
5. Constantine I. *Centenionalis. CONSTANTINVS AVG — SARMATIA DEVICTA.* RIC VII (Trier) 435 (323-4).
6. Constantine I. *Centenionalis. CONSTANTINVS AVG — CONSTANTINI MAX AVG.* RIC VII (Arles) 233 (321).
7. Crispus, Caesar (317-26). *Centenionalis. IVL CRISPVS NOB C — CAESARVM NOSTRORVM.* RIC VII (Lyons) 215 (323-4).
8. Constantine II, Caesar (317-37). *Centenionalis. CONSTANTINVS IVN NOB C PROVIDENTIAE CAESS.* RIC VII (Trier) 505 (327-8).
9. Constantine I (307-37) *Centenionalis. CONSTANTINVS MAX AVG — GLORIA EXERCITVS.* LRBC I 1356 (330-5).
10. Constantine II. *Centenionalis. FL MAX THEODORAE AVG — PIETAS ROMANA.* LRBC I 113 (337-41).

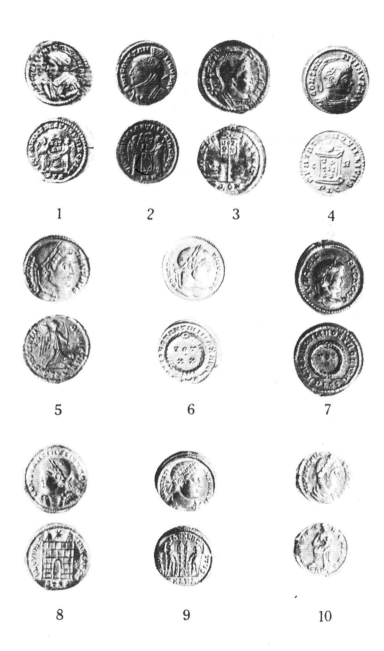

1   2   3   4

5   6   7

8   9   10

to coincide with the eleven hundredth anniversary of the foundation of the city of Rome, a comprehensive revision of the billon issues was undertaken. In keeping with the occasion, all denominations of the new coinage bore a single optimistic legend, *FEL(IX) TEMP(ORUM) REPARATIO* (The restoration of happy times). Three denominations were issued; the largest, weighing 5.2 grams, contained three and a half per cent silver, the intermediate coin was struck at 4.5 grams and contained one and a half per cent silver and the third, weighing 2.6 grams, contained no silver at all (plate 6 nos. 1-4). The intended relationship between the largest coin and the other two appears to have been 1: ½: ⅓. The manner in which the new billon coins related to the *solidus* and the silver coinage is unknown. It is probable that the new coin was known as the *maiorina* ('the big one'). The relative value of gold and silver fluctuated from time to time so that the exchange rate between gold and silver coins was subject to market forces. In the following table an attempt has been made, using a gold to silver ratio of 1:14.5, to establish the minimum number of silver coins to the *solidus*. Silver coins were usually issued at a weight lighter than the theoretical standard and at an unrealistically overvalued rate.

Late Roman silver coinage: denominations (plate 5 nos. 1-7) (after Kent)

Intended fraction of Roman pound	average weight	period of issue					Minimum number to solidus
1/24	12.6 g	—	337-58	358-95	—	—	5
1/60	5.2 g	—	337-58	358-95	—	402-500	12
1/72	4.4 g	325-37	337-58	358-95	395-402	402-500	14
1/96	3.4 g	325-37	—	—	—	—	19
1/144	2.2 g	—	—	358-95	—	402-500	29
1/192	1.7 g	—	—	—	395-402	—	38
1/300	1.1 g	—	—	358-95	—	402-500	60

Plate 5. FOURTH-CENTURY SILVER COINAGE
1. Constans (337-50). *Miliarense. FL IVL CONSTANS PF AVG — VIRTVS DD NN AVGG.* C 189 Trier (*c* 337). Weight 5 grams.
2. Constans. *Siliqua. CONSTANS PF AVG — CONSTANS AVG.* C 1 var Siscia (*c* 338). Weight 3.15 grams.
3. Constantius II (337-61). *Miliarense. DN CONSTANTIVS PF AVG — VIRTVS EXERCITVS.* C 342, Sirmium (352-3). Weight 4.4 grams.
4. Constantius II. *Siliqua. DN CONSTANTIVS PF AVG — VOTIS XXX MVLTIS XXXX.* C 342, Sirmium (352-3). Weight 2.9 grams.
5. Constantius II. *Siliqua. DN CONSTANTIVS PF AVG — VOTIS XXX MVLTIS XXXX.* C 341, Lyons (353-4). Weight 1.96 grams.
6. Magnus Maximus (383-8). *Siliqua. DN MAG MAXIMVS PF AVG — VIRTVS ROMANORVM.* RIC IX (Trier) 84b. Weight 1.97 grams.
7. Honorius (393-423). *Siliqua. DN HONORIVS PF AVG — VIRTVS ROMANORVM.* RIC IX (Milan) 32 (395). Weight 1.5 grams.

1

2

3

4

5

6

7

The coinage of the *Fel Temp Reparatio* reform suffered the usual fate of the billon coinage and very rapid depreciation took place. By 361 the largest coin of the series was the only extant remnant of the reformed system and this weighed a mere 2.2 grams. After 353 the addition of silver to the coin appears to have ceased (plate 6 no. 5).

Hitherto the eastern and the western halves of the Empire, under the rule of the sons of Constantine the Great, had acted uniformly in matters of monetary affairs. However, in 350, this unity was interrupted by a revolt in Gaul which brought to the western throne a usurper, Magnentius. The revolt was crushed after three years, but towards the end of his reign Magnentius abandoned the issue of billon coinage, which he had struck at the same standard as the legitimate *Fel Temp Reparatio* issues though with different types (plate 6 nos. 6-8). He thus anticipated by a short period the same action by Constantius. The suppression of Magnentius was to have a profound effect on the coinage circulating in Britain and Gaul, the areas which had been the base of his brief power.

Intermittent attempts were made to remedy the defect in the currency system brought on by the collapse of the *Fel Temp Reparatio* series. Julian (360-3) attempted to re-establish a Diocletianic standard with the introduction of an 8.3 gram billon coin containing three per cent silver. This coin, with its blatantly pagan reverse type of an Apis bull, hardly survived the death of Julian in battle in Persia (plate 7 no. 1). What did survive was a bronze fraction, originally issued by the Rome mint, at a weight standard of 2.4 grams (plate 7 no. 2). This denomination was produced in huge numbers by the succeeding dynasty of Valentinian (364-75). Any attempt to introduce an element of silver into the small-change system was now finally abandoned. Henceforth the currency metals consisted of gold,

Plate 6. THE *FEL TEMP REPARATIO* REFORM
1. Constantius II (337-61). *DN CONSTANTIVS PF AVG — FEL TEMP REPARATIO.* LRBC 2 38. Trier (348).
2. Constantius II. *DN CONSTANTIVS PF AVG — FEL TEMP REPARATIO.* LRBC 2 2486. Cyzicus (351).
3. Constans (337-50). *DN CONSTANS PF AVG — FEL TEMP REPARATIO.* LRBC 2 179. Lyons (348).
4. Constans. *DN CONSTANS PF AVG — FEL TEMP REPARATIO.* LRBC 2 33. Trier (348).
5. Constantius Gallus, Caesar (351-4). *DN CONSTANTIVS NOB CAES — FEL TEMP REPARATIO.* LRBC 2 2845. Alexandria (354).
6. Magnentius (350-3). *DN MAGNENTIVS PF AVG — FELICITAS REIPVBLICE.* LRBC 2 209. Lyons (350).
7. Magnentius. *DN MAGNENTIVS PF AVG — GLORIA ROMANORVM.* LRBC 2 429. Arles (351).
8. Magnentius. *DN MAGNENTIVS PF AVG — VICTORIAE DD NN AVG ET CAES.* LRBC 2 58. Trier (351).

1   2   3

4   5

6   7   8

silver and leaded bronze.

Even though reduced to base metal, the subsidiary coinage underwent further changes before the close of the fourth century. In *c* 380, Gratian (375-83) and his eastern co-emperor, Valentinian II (375-92), issued a multiple of the 2.4 gram coin weighing about 5.25 grams and thus perhaps intended as a double unit (plate 7 no. 3). A fraction was also issued, intended as a quarter of the new coin, weighing 1.5 grams (plate 7 no. 4). In the western half of the Empire the larger and intermediate denominations did not outlast 388, so that only the 1.5 gram issue remained. In the east the larger denominations survived longer but did not reach the west (plate 7 no. 5). The relationship of these coins to the *solidus* and silver is uncertain but it is clear that individually they represented many notional *denarii* and that several thousand represented a single *solidus*. In any event, the weight of the copper *nummus* continued to drop in the last decade of the fourth century until, at the date at which the mints of the Western Empire, with the exception of Rome, ceased to strike bronze coinage in 402, it weighed little more than 1 gram (plate 7 no. 6). It was at this standard, or a little less, that the spasmodic bronze coinage of the fifth century was issued, until the comprehensive reform of the emperor Anastasius in 498.

Plate 7. DENOMINATIONS: LATER FOURTH CENTURY
1. Julian (360-3). *DN FL CL IVLIANVS PF AVG — SECVRITAS REIPVB.* LRBC 2 468. Arles (361-3).
2. Julian. *DN FL CL IVLIANVS PF AVG — VOT X MVLT XX.* LRBC 2 695. Rome (360-3).
3. Gratian (367-83). *DN GRATIANVS PF AVG — REPARATIO REIPVB.* LRBC 2 376. Lyons (378-83).
4. Gratian. *DN GRATIANVS PF AVG — VOT XV MVLT XX.* LRBC 2 378. Lyons (378-83).
5. Theodosius I (379-95). *DN THEODOSIVS PF AVG — VIRTVS EXERCITI.* LRBC 2 2894. Alexandria (383-92).
6. Galla Placidia (421-50). *DN GALLA PLACIDIA PF AVG — SALVS REIPVBLICAE.* LRBC 2 854. Rome (425-50).

1

2

3

4

5

6

2
The Roman coinage in Britain

The discussion of Roman coinage in relation to even a small area of the Empire is fraught with difficulties. Within the Empire as a whole there are broad variations in the volume of coinage which, from time to time, makes up the currency pool. Variables, in antiquity, would include the physical richness of the area, the manner in which it was exploited and the activity of armies, both Roman and hostile, within the area. In general the Eastern Empire was always richer than the Western, but the West and Balkan regions deployed the largest armies and had frequently to withstand the incursions of hostile forces from beyond the frontiers. Britain, at the very extremity of the Roman world, presents a microcosm of the whole. It deployed a very large standing army and suffered attacks from across its provincial frontiers or by maritime raiders. Geographical factors effectively divided Britain into two zones, one of which was relatively rich and abounded in towns, cities and settlements, the other being the preserve of a scanty rural pastoral population and the standing army. Microcosm though it may be, Britain does not have a currency pattern which is necessarily uniform with any other area of the Empire. Although the events which shaped provinces tend to be similar, the rate and date of these events are variable, and the response of the provincials differed from place to place. Furthermore, a coinage which ultimately reflected the needs of a centralised imperial administration was not necessarily manipulated for the benefit of the component parts of the Empire. Indeed, as will be seen, there were times when the administration of the Roman coinage ran contrary to the needs of its provincial users.

There are other grave limitations on the deductions which may be legitimately drawn from coin evidence. To their original possessors coins represented health, wealth and the pursuit of happiness; to modern scholars they represent, all too often, economic or chronological abstractions. It is in the light of their original status that their later utility must be measured. In general coins were not thrown away and the life of the individual coin in circulation might have been very long, at least as long, for some denominations, as Britain's pre-decimal currency. This factor can be measured on the Antonine Wall, a structure occupied between c 140 and c 165, or later, and where pre-Antonine coinage is

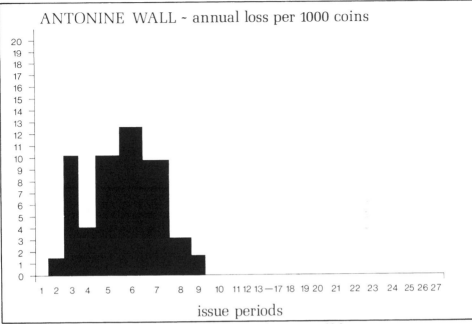

Fig. 3. Coin losses: Antonine Wall sites. For explanation see pages 28-9.

dominant (fig. 3). Coins from site finds, as opposed to hoards, generally represent what their owners could best afford to lose: those of high value — *aurei, solidi* and silver — will have been searched for most assiduously when dropped. Coins of little intrinsic worth (the ancient equivalent of new halfpennies) are abundant because they were worth much less effort to recover. Similarly larger coins are scarcer than small ones because they are more easily recovered and losses in the home are more often found again than those in, say, the market place.

Even when large numbers of coins are recovered from archaeological sites they rarely amount to very much in monetary terms. The site of Corstopitum (Corbridge in Northumberland) was important throughout the Roman period, first as a fort and later as a large urban centre. More than fifty years of excavations have produced 1387 coins of the first and second centuries, the period during which the site was a regular garrisoned fort. These coins, representing one hundred and twenty years of occupation, are the equivalent of twenty-six *aurei*. Over this period of nearly a century and a quarter the garrison varied in composition but if we assume that it was held by never less than a cohort of five hundred infantry (at times it was garrisoned by higher paid cavalry) who were paid at the standard rate of four *aurei* a man per year, we can calculate that our total coin finds represent a real coin population of at least 240,000 *aurei* or 24,000,000 *sestertii*. Conclusions drawn from such a tiny percentage of recovered data must be used with caution.

SITE FINDS: CIVIL SITES

The study of finds from individual sites indicates that there is a strongly marked pattern in the coinage of Roman Britain. Analysis of the component parts of this pattern makes it clear that it reflects factors other than the fate or status of individual sites; what we see reflected are largely monetary and political events.

The best places to study this pattern are in the major towns of Roman Britain which have been explored over a long period, which have produced large numbers of coins and whose upper levels have not been eroded by post-Roman developments. Whatever the problems affecting coin losses in antiquity, we can expect them to have operated uniformly so that we may postulate that the loss from the original coin population will have always been roughly constant in relation to the coins in circulation in any period. We can also asume that for sites with very long coin lists a cross sample has been recovered which is representative of the original coin population, albeit of the lower denominations. To make valid comparisons from site to site the various totals of coins from different sites must be presented on a single statistical basis and account must be taken of the varying lengths of time during which individual coins, or series of coins, were issued. It would, for instance, be inappropriate to compare directly the coinage of a long reign with that of a short one and make deductions based upon the disparate numbers of coins in each period. The way around this problem is to express all coins on a single numerical basis; in practice one of a thousand notional coins has been found to be a convenient figure from which a histogram can be constructed. All coins are then expressed by the formula:

$$\frac{\text{coins per period}}{\text{length of period}} \quad \text{x} \quad \frac{1,000}{\text{total for site}}$$

Periods are sometimes the reigns of individual rulers, at other times the issue life of important elements in the currency.

Coin periods

period	date range	principal rulers
1. Claudian	43-54	Claudius
2. Neronian	54-68	Nero
3. Flavian I	68-81	Vespasian, Titus
4. Flavian II	81-96	Domitian
5. Trajanic	96-117	Nerva, Trajan
6. Hadrianic	117-38	Hadrian
7. Antonine I	138-61	Antoninus Pius
8. Antonine II	161-80	Marcus Aurelius
9. Antonine III	180-92	Commodus
10. Severan I	193-217	Septimus Severus, Caracalla
11-17. Severan II	217-60	Elagabalus, Severus Alexander, Maximinus, Gordian III, Philip, Decius, Gallus, Valerian
18. Gallic Empire	260-73	Postumus, Victorinus, Tetricus, Gallienus
19. Aurelianic	273-86	Aurelian, Tacitus, Probus, Carinus
20. Carausian	286-96	Carausius, Allectus
21. Diocletianic	296-317	Diocletian, Maximian, Constantius, Galerius, Constantine I
22. Constantinian I	317-30	Constantine I, Licinius
23. Constantinian II	330-48	Constantine I, Constantine II, Constans, Constantius II
24. Constantinian III	348-64	Constantius II, Magnentius, Julian
25. Valentinianic	364-78	Valentinian I, Valens, Gratian
26. Theodosian I	378-88	Gratian, Theodosius I, Magnus Maximus
27. Theodosian II	388-402	Theodosius I, Honorius, Arcadius

(For convenience of computation, pre-Claudian coins are omitted as well as all copies, except Claudian.)

Application of this formula to a number of very productive town sites shows that there are periods at which coins are very abundant and others in which they are very scarce (figs. 4-6). It can hardly be that these towns all suffer exactly the same periodic disturbances in their economic affairs,

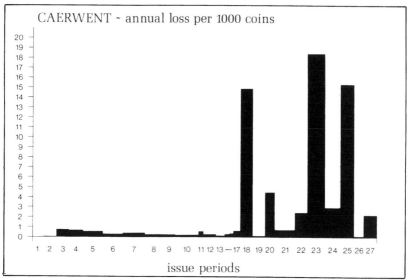

Fig. 4. Coin losses: Caerwent (Venta Silurum).

so that it follows that there are reasons for the fluctuations which are inherent in the nature of the coins themselves or that they are the result of generally operating factors. Most of the fluctuations can be ascribed to changes in the imperial currency system or to political events.

Period 1: Claudian (43-54)

Early coinage is not usually well represented both because of the inevitably slow initial growth of sites and because early levels are relatively less well explored than later levels. The presence of a military garrison can usually be detected by an abnormally large number of early coins, for instance at Wroxeter, which served as a legionary base in the Neronian to early Flavian periods. Claudian coinage suffers from a very low emission rate, with virtually no imperial coinage reaching Britain after *c* 44. This problem is further exacerbated by the Senate's attempted suppression of the coinage of Claudius' predecessor Gaius (Caligula), with the exception of coins struck by him in the name of Agrippa, his grandfather (plate 8 no. 1).

Dominant types. *Asses,* Minerva type (plate 8 no. 2). *Dupondii,* Ceres (plate 8 no. 3).

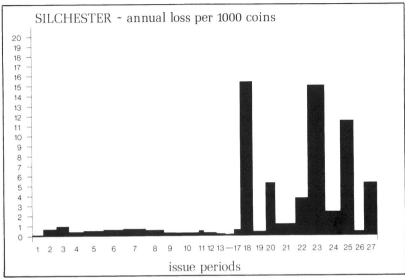

Fig. 5. Coin losses: Silchester (Calleva Atrebatum).

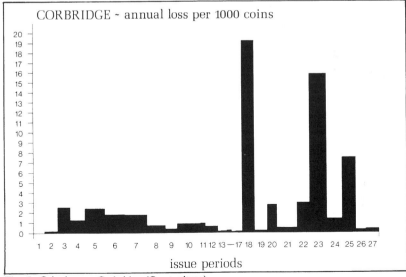

Fig. 6. Coin losses: Corbridge (Corstopitum).

Period 2: Neronian (54-68)

The absence of new issues from the middle of the reign of Claudius intensified in the reign of Nero, who issued no *orichalcum* or copper coins between his accession in 54 and 64. This ten-year gap was filled in provinces with well established coinage pools by recirculating and retariffing very worn coins from earlier periods. Britain, which had only recently come under the domination of Rome, had no such resources. From the middle of Claudius' reign until the resumption of coining by Nero a series of copies of Claudius' coins circulated in Britain and Gaul, from which many may have been imported. These 'Claudian copies' range in style from close approximations to the original down to miserable productions of execrable style and low weight. Most of these unofficial issues, perhaps all but the very best copies, date to the reign of Nero. They are characteristic finds on sites associated with Neronian military activity but are also found on civil sites. Clearly the copies were widely accepted and filled a considerable need. The resumption of official coinage in 64 alleviated the shortage, but the coins which had served during the fiscal crisis continued to circulate for some time after their production ceased.

Dominant types. *Asses* (a) Minerva copies (plate 8 nos. 4-5), (b) Victory flying left holding shield — after AD 64 (plate 8 no. 6).

Periods 3-4: Flavian (68-96)

The advent of the Flavian dynasty brought a new vigour to Britain after a period of unsettlement and indecision created by political events in Rome itself. A powerful drive to complete the conquest was initiated and troops, hitherto stationed in the south, were moved north. The growth of urban communities took on renewed impetus. A large volume of coinage reached Britain to finance these events, including silver, often comprising very worn issues of the Republic.

Dominant types. Vespasian: *dupondii/asses* (a) *FELICITAS PVBLICA*

Plate 8. JULIO-CLAUDIAN COIN TYPES
1. Agrippa. *As. M AGRIPPA L F COS III* — Neptune SC. RIC 32.
2. Claudius (41-54). *As. TI CLAVDIVS CAESAR AVG PM TR P IMP PP* — Minerva SC. RIC 66.
3. Claudius. *Dupondius. TI CLAVDIVS CAESAR AVG PM TR P IMP PP* — *CERES AVGVSTA SC.* RIC 67.
4. 'Claudius'. *As.* Minerva copy.
5. 'Claudius'. *As.* Minerva copy.
6. Nero (54-68). *As. IMP NERO CAESAR AVG P MAX TR P PP* — Victory flying SC. RIC 329.

1 2 3

4 5 6

(plate 9 no. 1), (b) eagle on globe (plate 9 no. 2), (c) *AEQVITAS AVGVSTI* (plate 9 no. 3). Domitian: *dupondii/asses* (a) *FORTVNAE AVGVSTI* (plate 9 no. 4), (b) *MONETA AVGVSTI* (plate 9 no. 5), (c) *VIRTVTI AVGVSTI* (plate 9 no. 6). Republic: *denarii.* M. Antonius — galley (plate 10 no. 1).

Periods 5-8: Trajanic, Hadrianic and Antonine I and II (96-180)

A transition in the value of denominations took place in the second century with the *sestertius* dominating the coinage, though *asses* and, particularly, *dupondii* continued to play a large part in day-to-day transactions. By the middle of the reign of Marcus Aurelius the volume of *aes* coinage fell very sharply. Military pressures caused a debasement of the *denarius,* and it began to assume a dominant role in the coinage.

Dominant types. Trajan: (a) *sestertii SPQR OPTIMO PRINCIPI* (with personification) (plate 10 no. 2). Antoninus Pius: (a) *as BRITANNIA COS IIII* (Britannia seated in dejected pose) — especially frequent in association with northern military sites (plate 10 no. 3). Faustina I Deified: (a) *sestertii DIVA FAVSTINA* (plate 10 no. 4).

Periods 9-17: Antonine III and Severan (180-260)

The periods from the middle of the reign of Marcus Aurelius to the middle of the third century are ones in which the currency system underwent systematic debasement. *Denarii* fell in weight and fineness by stages through the reigns of Marcus Aurelius and Commodus (fig. 2), reaching a tariff of fifty per cent silver in the reign of Severus, whose financial problems partly arose from his raising military pay (plate 10 nos. 5-7). In the early periods of this phase of the coinage *aes* gave way to silver, with consequent effects on the volume of site finds attributable to issues of these decades. Earlier coinage continued to cir-

Plate 9. FLAVIAN COIN TYPES
  1. Vespasian (69-79). *Dupondius. IMP CAES VESP AVG PM TR P COS VI — FELICITAS PVBLICA SC.* RIC 567 75.
  2. Vespasian. *As. IMP CAES VESPASIAN AVG COS VIII PP* — Eagle on globe. RIC 364b. Lyons (77-9).
  3. Vespasian. *As. IMP CAES VESPASIAN AVG COS VIII PP — AEQVITAS AVGVSTI SC.* RIC 758 (77-9).
  4. Domitian (81-96). *Dupondius. IMP CAES DOMIT AVG GERM COS XVI CENS PERP P — FORTVNAE AVGVSTI SC.* RIC 405 (92-4).
  5. Domitian. *As. IMP CAES DOMIT AVG GERM COS XIII CENS PERP P — MONETA AVGVSTI SC.* RIC 354a (87).
  6. Domitian. *Dupondius. IMP CAES DOMITIAN AVG GERM COS XI — VIRTVTI AVGVSTI SC.* RIC 305a var. (85).

1   2   3

4   5   6

culate in profusion until the middle of the third century. Since a single *denarius* represented the purchasing power of four *sestertii* or sixteen *asses*, there were proportionally less currency units to be lost. The effect of a debasement of the silver coinage was to drive earlier silver out of circulation. Silver of the early third century is marginally more common, especially in military contexts, than that of the middle of the century, by which time the coin of commerce had changed from the *denarius* to the *antoninianus*. A great deal of Severan silver proves, on close examination, to be counterfeit, perhaps indicating that it was produced at a period when relatively good Severan *denarii* stood at a premium. Against the trend a persistently high number of *denarii* of Severus Alexander (222-34) are found (Period 11), possibly indicative of some unrecorded military event in Britain at this date, though the general trend for Britain in the third century differs from this interpretation (plate 10 no. 8).

The general shift in the strategic balance of the Empire was towards the Danube region, with the result that Britain became a military backwater for most of the century. A reduction in the garrison probably took place and thus a decline in the flow of new coin as military pay. A problem of great magnitude, in relation to the interpretation of coin finds, arises in this period. We have seen that after the re-establishment of the denomination, the *antoninianus* coinage underwent systematic debasement. The result of this was twofold; the withdrawal of better coin by the state to furnish the raw material to produce worse, and the conversion of relatively good coin into hoards or plate by private owners. This withdrawal accelerated as the intrinsic value of the coinage declined. Very little appears to have escaped these processes to make any great impact as site finds. In these circumstances it would be wrong to use the decline in the coin finds at this period as evidence for the abandonment or decline of individual sites (figs. 4-6).

Plate 10. COIN TYPES, SECOND AND THIRD CENTURIES
1. Marcus Antonius. *Denarius. ANT AVG III VIR RPC — LEG VI.* S 33.
2. Trajan (98-117). *Sestertius. IMP CAES NERVA TRAIANO AVG GER DAC PM TR P COS V PP — SPQR OPTIMO PRINCIPI SC.* RIC 506 (103-11).
3. Antoninus Pius (138-61). *As. ANTONINVS AVG PIVS PP TR P XVIII — BRITANNIA COS IIII SC.* RIC 934 (154-5).
4. Faustina I. *Sestertius. DIVA FAVSTINA — AVGVSTA SC.* RIC (Ant Pius) 1125.
5. Septimus Severus (193-211). *Denarius. SEVERVS PIVS AVG — PM TR P XIII COS III PP.* RIC 196 (205).
6. Julia Domna. *Denarius. IVLIA DOMNA AVG — VENERI VICTR.* RIC 536 (193-6).
7. Caracalla (196-218). *Denarius. ANTONINVS PIVS AVG — VICT PART MAX.* RIC 144(b) (201-6).
8. Severus Alexander (222-35). *Denarius. IMP ALEXAND PIVS AVG — MARS VLTOR.* RIC 246 (231-5).

Period 18: Gallic Empire (260-73)

The uniformly high number of coins of this period reflects the collapse of the imperial currency system. The coin finds consist exclusively of the base double *denarii* of the Gallic Empire and issues of its legitimate rivals. The decline in the coinage is reflected not only in the huge numbers recorded as site finds throughout the Empire but also in the opening up of new mints, or the expansion of existing ones, for its production. In a period of inflation an increase in the number of coins in circulation does not indicate prosperity, but quite the contrary, since the larger volume of coinage is used to pay for an unchanged amount of goods and services.

Dominant types. Gallienus: *antoniniani APOLLINI/DIANAE CONS AVG* (plate 11 nos. 1-2). Victorinus: *antoniniani PAX AVG/INVICTVS* (plate 11 nos. 3-4). Tetricus I: *antoniniani PAX AVG* (plate 11 no. 5). Tetricus II: *antoniniani SPES AVGG/SPES PVBLICA/PIETAS AVGVSTOR* (plate 11 nos. 6-7). Claudius II, posthumous: *CONSECRATIO* (altar)/*CONSECRATIO* (eagle) (plate 11 nos. 8-9).

Period 19: Aurelianic (273-86)

From the recovery of the Empire by Aurelian the Roman currency shows the effects of a series of reforms and depreciations. Period 19 coincides with the reform of 273 and the issue of the XXI billon coinage by Aurelian and his successors, who sought to stabilise in monetary affairs after the financial disaster of the previous decades. Coins of the reform are very scarce and this is not surprising if they bore a tariff of five *denarii*; further, the possibility exists that many of these coins were restruck in the reign of Carausius. In any event, the shortage of coinage was remedied in Britain and Gaul, and other provinces to a lesser extent, by the wholesale production of copies of the coinage of the Gallic Empire,

Plate 11. THE GALLIC EMPIRE
1. Gallienus (258-68). *Antoninianus. IMP GALLIENVS AVG — APOLLINI CONS AVG.* RIC 165.
2. Gallienus. *Antoninianus. IMP GALLIENVS AVG — DIANAE CONS AVG.* RIC 176.
3. Victorinus (268-70). *Antoninianus. IMP C VICTORINVS PF AVG — PAX AVG.* RIC 118.
4. Victorinus. *Antoninianus. IMP C VICTORINVS PF AVG — INVICTVS.* RIC 114.
5. Tetricus I (270-3). *Antoninianus. IMP C TETRICVS PF AVG — PAX AVG.* RIC 180.
6. Tetricus II. *Antoninianus. C PIV ESV TETRICVS CAES — SPES AVGG.* RIC 270.
7. Tetricus II (270-3). *Antoninianus. C P E TETRICVS CAES — PIETAS AVGVSTOR.* RIC 258.
8. Claudius II (268-70), deified. *Antoninianus. DIVO CLAVDIO — CONSECRATIO* (altar). RIC 259.
9. Claudius II, deified. *Antoninianus. DIVO CLAVDIO — CONSECRATIO* (eagle). RIC 266.

1

2

3

4

5

6

7

8 9

with prototypes of Tetricus overwhelmingly dominating these issues (plate 12 nos. 1-7). Radiate copies (the older literature refers to these coins as 'barbarous radiates') appear to have been produced between *c* 273 and *c* 282. Attempts have been made to establish a chronology of coins based upon size, with the largest copies standing closest to their prototypes and the smallest (14-8 millimetres diameter) at the extremity of the series. The latest detectable prototype for radiate copies is to be found in the coinage of Probus (276-82). Their general circulation may well have ceased in 286 with the accession of Carausius. The ability of the producers of radiate copies to imitate their prototypes varies with time, the earliest issues being reasonably close to the coins copied, though frequently illiteracy is demonstrated by the miscopying of inscriptions. As copies were produced based not on genuine coins but on previous generations of copies, so legends become more garbled and the types become more and more abstract and disintegrated. Some elements remain constant even in the worst copies, especially the emphasis on the depiction of the emperor's radiate crown. Radiate copies occur on both civil and military sites and are found hoarded with orthodox coins. Evidently such copies filled a substantial gap in the Aurelianic reformed coinage system.

Period 20: Carausian (286-96)

It is only with the arrival of the usurper Carausius in 286 that Britain once again displays an abundance of coinage. The observed volume may be credited to the usurper's need to inject a large number of coins into the island's economy as donatives intended to secure the loyalty of the army. On the other hand, the volume may be illusory since Carausian coinage and that of his successor and murderer, Allectus, were almost certainly demonetised when Britain was recovered by the Empire in 296, a date which coincides with the implementation of Diocletian's reforms. The Carausian billon coinage was produced on the Aurelianic standard and was accompanied by issues in high-grade silver of unknown denomination

Plate 12. RADIATE COPIES AND LATE THIRD-CENTURY TYPES
1. 'Gallienus'. *'FELICIT AVG'* copy of RIC 187.
2. 'Tetricus I'. *'PAX AVG'* copy of RIC 180.
3. 'Tetricus I'. *'VIRTVS AVG'* copy of RIC 146.
4. 'Tetricus I'. *'TVTELA'* copy of RIC 137.
5. 'Tetricus II'. *'HILARITAS AVGG'* copy of RIC 232.
6. 'Tetricus II'. *'PRINC IVVENT'* copy of RIC 260.
7. 'Tetricus I'. *'PAX AVG'* copy of RIC 180.
8. Carausius (286-93). *Aureus. CARAVSIVS PF AVG — CONSERVAT AVG.* RIC 1 var.
9. Carausius. *'Denarius'. IMP CARAVSIVS PF AVG — EXPECTATE VENI.* RIC 771.

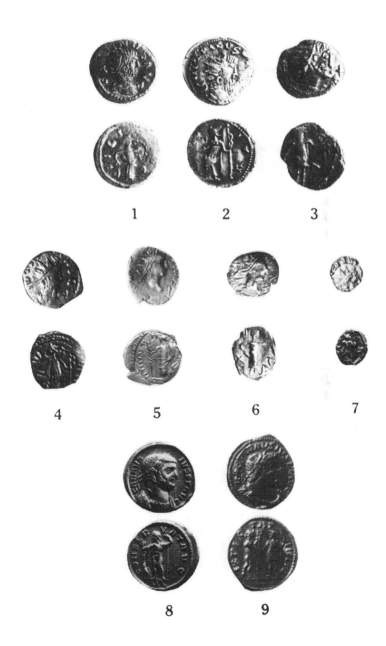

1   2   3

4   5   6   7

8   9

and *aurei* (plate 12 nos. 8-9).

Dominant types. Carausius: *'antoniniani' PAX AVG/AVGGG* (plate 13 nos. 1-2). Allectus: *'antoniniani' PAX AVG/PROVID[ENTIA]AVG* (plate 13 nos. 3-4); *quinarii VIRTVS AVG/LAETITIA AVG* (plate 13 nos. 5-6).

Period 21: Diocletianic (296-317)

Diocletian's reformed coinage is very rare. The 10-gram *'follis'*, of silver-surfaced billon, was of high unitary value and of a module that made the recovery of mislaid specimens both desirable and relatively easy. Almost all of the coins recorded as site finds of this period are of the later Constantinian issues of diminished module and intrinsic value.

Dominant types. Diocletian, Maximian and colleagues: *'folles' GENIO POPVLI ROMANI* (plate 13 no. 7). Constantine and colleagues: *'folles'* (a) *GENIO POP ROM* (plate 3 no. 6), (b) *SOLI INVICTO COMITI* (plate 13 no. 8).

Periods 22-3: Constantinian I and II (317-48)

It was Constantine's monetary policy periodically to debase the billon issues. As the coinage declined towards its final 1.5 gram module, reached in the last years of Constantine and maintained by his sons, so the volume of coinage increases. The minor value of these issues is emphasised by their frequency and by the attempt at reform in 348. Successive depreciations led to the selective hoarding of previous issues. The place of the stabilised gold coinage of this period, never represented in site finds, as a commodity, allowed for the inflation of the minor denominations without serious damage to the state's finances.

The relative unimportance of this coinage in the eyes of the state is

Plate 13. COIN TYPES: LATE THIRD CENTURY
1. Carausius (286-93). *'Antoninianus'. IMP CARAVSIVS PF AVG — PAX AVG.* RIC 121.
2. Carausius. *'Antoninianus'. IMP C CARAVSIVS PF AVG — PAX AVGGG.* RIC 143.
3. Allectus (293-6). *'Antoninianus'. IMP C ALLECTVS PF AVG — PAX AVG.* RIC 28.
4. Allectus. *'Antoninianus'. IMP C ALLECTVS PF AVG — PROVID AVG.* RIC 36.
5. Allectus. *'Quinarius'. IMP C ALLECTVS PF AVG — LAETITIA AVG.* RIC 125.
6. Allectus. *'Quinarius'. IMP C ALLECTVS PF AVG — VIRTVS AVG.* RIC 128.
7. Constantius I, Caesar. *'Follis'. FL VAL CONSTANTIVS NOB C — GENIO POPVLI ROMANI.* RIC VI (Rome) 66a (296-7).
8. Constantine I (307-37). *'Follis'. IMP CONSTANTINVS PF AVG — SOLI INVICTO COMITI.* RIC VII (Arles) 57 (315-6).

1

2

3

4

5

6

7

8

exemplified by an hiatus in the supply of coinage which occurred between *c* 341 and 346. This shortfall was made good by the production of copies, in a variety of degrees of competence, of the extant *GLORIA EXER-CITVS, VRBS ROMA* and *CONSTANTINOPOLIS* coinages (plate 14 nos. 6-7).

Dominant types. Period 22: (a) *VICTORIAE LAETAE PRINC PERP* (plate 4 no. 2), (b) *BEATA TRANQVILLITAS* (plate 4 no. 4), (c) *CAESARVM NOSTRORVM* (plate 4 no. 7). Period 23: (a) *GLORIA EXERCITVS* — two standards (plate 14 no. 1), (b)*VRBS ROMA* (plate 14 no. 2), (c) *CONSTANTINOPOLIS* (plate 14 no. 3), (d) *GLORIA EXERCITVS* — one standard (plate 14 no. 4), (e) *VIC-TORIAE DD AVGG Q NN* (plate 14 no. 5), (f) issues for Helena and Theodora (plate 14 no. 8).

Period 24: Constantinian III (348-64)

Constans' and Constantius' reform of 348 brought back into circulation a high-value coinage comparable in module, and thus in site behaviour, with the *'folles'* of Diocletian. The relative dearth of these coins is a response, then, to their intrinsic value, but another factor is operative on the deposit of this coinage. The revolt of Magnentius (350-3) produced a coinage which followed that of Constantius in module and alloy. With the suppression of this revolt, draconian measures were taken to suppress the coinage of the usurper. The results were apparently successful and the subsequent dearth of coinage was made good by the local production of copies of the very scarce post-353 issues of Constantius. These copies of the *FEL TEMP REPARATIO* 'falling horseman' coin are very common and appear to have been produced between 354 and 364. Like the radiate

Plate 14. LATE CONSTANTINIAN TYPES
1. Constantine II, Caesar (317-37). *CONSTANTINVS IVN NOB C — GLORIA EXER-CITVS.* LRBC 1 49.
2. Constantine I (307-37). *VRBS ROMA* — wolf and twins. LRBC 1 535.
3. Constantine I. *CONSTANTINOPOLIS* — victory on prow. LRBC 1 655.
4. Constantius II (337-61). *FL IVL CONSTANTIVS AVG — GLORIA EXERCITVS.* LRBC 1 126.
5. Constans (337-50). *CONSTANS PF AVG — VICTORIAE DD AVGG Q NN.* LRBC 1 147.
6. 'Constantine I'. '*VRBS ROMA* ' copy of LRBC 1 184.
7. 'Constantine I'. '*CONSTANTINOPOLIS*' copy of LRBC 1 356.
8. Theodora. *FL MAX THEODORAE AVG — PIETAS ROMANA.*LRBC 1 113.
9. 'Constantius II'. '*DN CONSTANTIVS PF AVG — FEL TEMP REPARATIO*'.
10. 'Constantius II'. '*DOM NOSTRORVM — FEL TEMP REPARATIO*'. Overstruck on Constantine I *Gloria exercitus.*

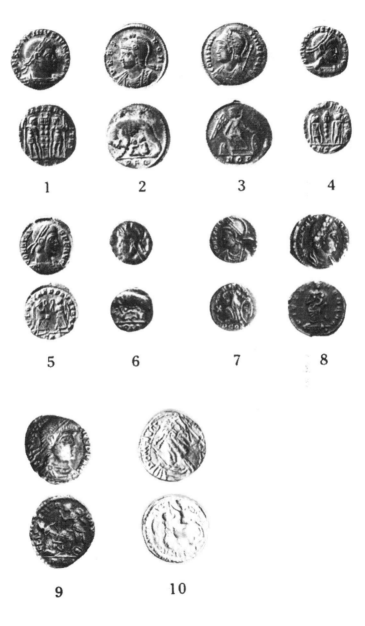

1   2   3   4

5   6   7   8

9   10

copies of the previous century, these unofficial issues rapidly declined in module and faithfulness to their prototype (plate 14 nos. 9-10).

Dominant types. *Centenionales.* Constans/Constantius II: *FEL TEMP REPARATIO* — hut/barbarian emperor/galley/phoenix (plate 6 nos. 1, 3-4). Constantius II: *FEL TEMP REPARATIO* — falling horseman (plate 6 no. 2). Magnentius, Decentius: *VICTORIAE DD NN AVG ET CAE* (plate 6 no. 8).

Period 25: Valentinianic (364-78)

The important role played by the issue of increasing numbers of *siliquae, miliarensia* and *solidi,* unrepresented in site finds, led to the abandonment of the billon series, which had had its origins in the troubles of the middle of the third century. The coinage of the house of Valentinian in bronze is very common and reflects its relatively low unit value and, perhaps, yet another upheaval in the fourth-century cycle of inflations which plagued the Roman world.

Dominant types. Valentinian, Valens: (a) *GLORIA ROMANORUM* (plate 15 no. 1), (b) *SECVRITAS REIPVBLICAE* (plate 15 no. 2). Gratian: *GLORIA NOVI SAECVLI* (plate 15 no. 3).

Period 26: Theodosian I (378-88)

The abrupt decline in coinage following the Valentinianic period requires explanation. Period 26 coincides with the revolt of Magnus

Plate 15. LATER FOURTH-CENTURY TYPES
1. Valens (364-78). *DN VALENS PF AVG — GLORIA ROMANORVM.* LRBC 2 989.
2. Valentinian I (364-75). *DN VALENTINIANVS PF AVG — SECVRITAS REIPV-BLICAE.* LRBC 2 996.
3. Gratian (367-83). *DN GRATIANVS AVGG AVG — GLORIA NOVI SAECVLI.* LRBC 2 529.
4. Valentinian II (375-92). *DN VALENTINIANVS PF AVG — VICTORIA AVGGG.* LRBC 2 390.
5. Valentinian II. *DN VALENTINIANVS PF AVG — VICTORIA AVGGG.* LRBC 2 1091.
6. Honorius (393-423). *DN HONORIVS PF AVG — SALVS REIPVBLICAE.* LRBC 2 1111.
7. Honorius. *DN HONORIVS PF AVG — VRBS ROMA FELIX.* LRBC 2 818. Rome (403-8).
8. Constantine III (406-11). *DN CONSTANTINVS PF AV — VICTORIA AAAVGGG.* C7: Lyons (c 408).
9. Julian, Caesar. Clipped *siliqua.* Weight 1.2 grams.
10. Honorius (393-423). *Solidus. DN HONORIVS PF AVG — VICTORIA AVGGG.* C 44: Milan (c 400).

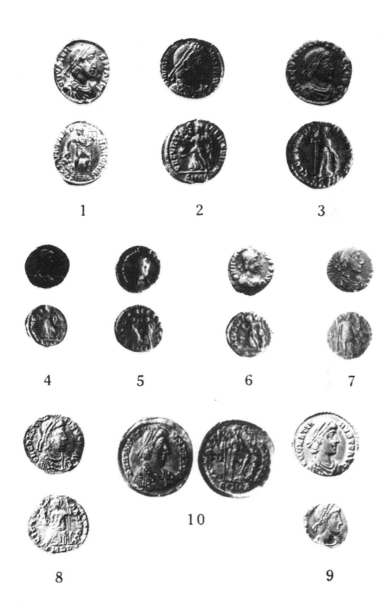

1   2   3

4   5   6   7

8   10   9

Maximus and a reform initiated by Gratian. Superficially attractive is the possibility that Maximus took the army of Britain to Gaul to support him in his claim to the throne and thus deprived Britain of the troops who would in the normal course of events have been issued with the new coinage. However, there is evidence which suggests that Maximus' usurpation had very little effect on the manning levels of the garrison of Britain. It may be that the high incidence of Valentinianic coin in circulation made new issues from the continent unnecessary, but such close monitoring of the small-change pool is not elsewhere in evidence. No copies were produced in this period, so that the lack of new coin cannot have created a small-change crisis as occurred in previous periods.

Period 27: Theodosian II (388-402)

The latest issues of Roman coinage which reached Britain in bulk were the AE4 module bronzes of the house of Theodosius. These coins emanated from the mints of Gaul until 395. With the closure of the Gallic mints, supplies for Britain were drawn from Rome and, to a lesser extent, Aquileia. The latest issues to arrive, in the names of Honorius and Arcadius, were of the *SALUS REIPVBLICAE* type. This coin was superseded in *c* 403 by a new issue bearing the legend *VRBS ROMA FELIX* (plate 15 no. 7). This new coinage did not reach Britain, hence it may be concluded that the payment of official salaries and the state's obligations entered into in Britain ceased in about 402. A small quantity of *solidi* and *siliquae* issued by the usurper Constantine III (406-11) have been found in Britain, both in site finds and in hoards (plate 15 no. 8). A few rare *siliquae* dating to 423 also occur as well as *siliquae* which have been severely clipped, a practice which started towards the end of the fourth century and extended into the fifth (plate 15 no. 9). Gold coinage follows the pattern of the bronze (plate 15 no. 10). A single bronze of Valentinian III, dating to *c* 435, is recorded from Wroxeter (Uriconium).

The abrupt cessation of the coin supply to Britain did not provoke any provision of local copies, a fact which seems to point to the extremely rapid collapse of the coin-dependent cash economy of Roman Britain.

Dominant types. Valentinian II, Theodosius, Arcadius, Honorius: (a) *VICTORIA AVGG/G* (plate 15 nos. 4-5), (b) *SALVS REIPVBLICAE* (plate 15 no. 6).

SITE FINDS: MILITARY SITES

The coins recovered from military sites are of the same issues as those found on civil sites. Since civil coinage may well be dependent, ultimately, on supplies circulated through the medium of the army, the composition of the currency in both classes of sites is similar. But there are a number of factors which affect the overall pattern of coinage associated with the army. In the first instance physical factors arise. Few military sites are as deeply stratified as town sites, so that the amount of coinage recoverable from earlier levels is generally greater. However, military sites were generally kept clean, so that there was always a factor operating against the future interests of the archaeologist. More important than this are considerations arising from the nature of military life itself. Forts were rarely occupied by the same unit for very long periods or by the same sorts of units. Differences in the pay structure of different kinds of soldiers — legionaries, auxiliary cavalry and auxiliary infantry — are complicating factors. So too are variations in the size of units — five thousand, one thousand or five hundred strong. In sum, the variations in unit size coupled with the mobility of the army make general deductions about military coinage very difficult to make with confidence. Were this not enough, there is the further complication of periodic rises in military pay. Soldiers' pay was always poor but had the advantage of being steady. It was raised on three occasions.

Basic pay (denarii per annum)

period	legionaries	auxiliary cavalry	part mounted auxiliaries	auxiliary infantry
Claudius-Domitian	225	—	—	—
Domitian-Severus	300	200	150	100
Severus-Caracalla	450	300	200	150
Caracalla	675	450	300	225

After the establishment of a northern frontier in Britain some units did settle down to long periods of residence in their forts. This is particularly true for the third and fourth centuries after the alarms and excursions of the advance to and retreat from the Antonine Wall and of Septimus Severus' unsuccessful campaigns designed to conquer the unsubdued areas of Caledonia. Settlements of dependents grew up around these forts, and it was in these *vici* that the soldiers spent such pay as remained after deductions had been made for food, equipment, retirement pay, the burial club and the unit's annual party at the Saturnalia. One site on the northern frontier which appears to have had a numerically stable garrison throughout its existence is the fort of Housesteads (Vercovicium) on Hadrian's Wall. It contained an auxiliary infantry unit, one thousand strong, from the reign of Hadrian until the late fourth or early fifth century. In the interval during which the Antonine Wall was held as the provincial frontier, Housesteads was held by legionary troops.

The coins from this site (fig. 7) present an interesting picture. Although the fort was founded in *c* 125, there is a considerable quantity of coinage of Trajan in the finds list, as well as of Antoninus Pius, from the period when the original garrison had moved on to Scotland and the higher paid legionaries had moved into their place. The increase in army pay given by Septimus Severus is well shown by a large representation of his coinage and that of his sons. This is followed by the normal decline in coins in the first half of the third century occasioned by the demise of the *denarius* and *antoninianus*. The complete collapse of the currency during the Gallic Empire (259-73) provides the majority of the coins of the third century.

Comparison of the coins found at Housesteads and other forts with those found at civil sites shows that the expectation of the numbers of coins to be found is a reverse pattern — large numbers of coins in the first, second and early third centuries on military sites, and relatively few on civil sites, and large numbers of coins in the fourth century in towns and relatively few in forts. It must be emphasised that the comparisons made are relative. Military sites with long occupation can have very large numbers of coins in absolute terms, but the early/late relationship is fairly constant; similar factors are applicable in considering civil sites.

The reason for this reverse pattern can be traced to the operation of the *annona militaris*. With the collapse of the currency system in the third century, the state began to levy taxes in kind, rather than in cash. Diocletian formalised the system and throughout the Empire taxation was estimated so as to supply the needs of the army and the imperial bureaucracy. Troops still received the same cash payments in terms of *denarii* as they had a hundred years previously when Caracalla raised their pay, but the bulk of their pay was in rations, equipment and weapons produced for them by the taxpayer. At third-century pay rates an auxiliary soldier in Diocletian's army would have received in cash only about sixty-eight *'folles'* per annum. This system persisted throughout the fourth

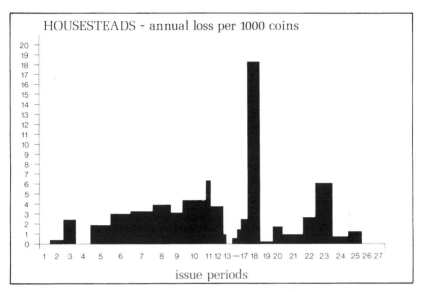

Fig. 7. Coin losses: Housesteads (Vercovicium).

century, the result being an acute diminution in the numbers of coins available to the troops and a consequent scarcity in the archaeological record. Naturally, the gold and silver coins presented to the soldiers on imperial accessions or celebrations do not normally find their way into the hands of archaeologists. By contrast the occurrence of gold coins in early military contexts is not entirely unknown in Britain, though such finds are of nugatory significance in relation to finds of small-change coinage.

Military sites, despite the effects of the *annona militaris*, can be expected to be the recipients of fresh coinage and so best demonstrate the results of the frequent changing of coin types. This rapid turnover in coins is well demonstrated in two groups of fourth-century military sites, the Yorkshire coast signal stations and the forts of the Saxon shore, where older coinage is virtually unknown (fig. 8).

COIN HOARDS

The hoarding instinct appears to be endemic; in all ages and all societies in which coins have been used hoarders are in evidence. Motives for

YORKSHIRE COAST SIGNAL STATIONS
annual loss per 100 coins

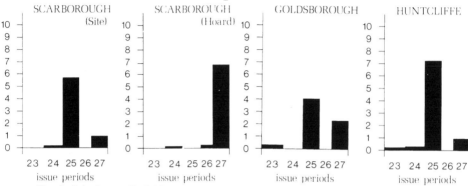

Fig. 8. Coin losses: Yorkshire coast signal stations.

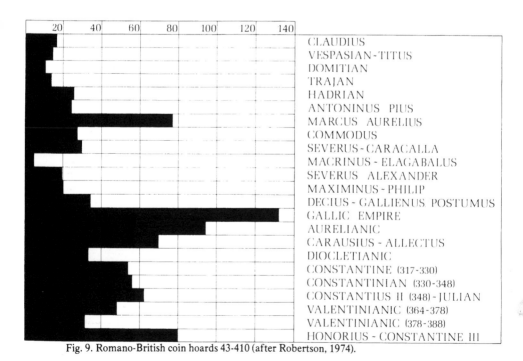

Fig. 9. Romano-British coin hoards 43-410 (after Robertson, 1974).

hoarding can vary greatly, but several elements can be distinguished: the concealment of available wealth in the face of some emergency, the slow accumulation of cash over a long period, and the deliberate hoarding of coins of high intrinsic value in periods of currency decline. The coins accumulated under the latter headings may, of course, have been deposited in the context of the first. Such an emergency does not need to have been as dramatic as barbarian raiding or native uprising, events all too frequently deduced, probably erroneously, from coin hoards, but from the simple exigencies of life in a society which was, on a day-to-day level, precarious. The preliminary to a journey, for instance, might have been the depositing of spare cash in a safe place, either on the premises or nearby. Most hoards, we may assume, were rapidly retrieved. Those that were not may have been abandoned by their owners because they had been rendered valueless or some event prevented their recovery. This event would usually be construed as the death of the depositor, but sheer bad luck in losing the landmark which located the hoard should not be overlooked.

In dealing with the historical or economic context of coin hoards the dating of the hoard is of crucial importance. Because the latest coin in a hoard only offers an earliest possible date, the contents of the hoard must be viewed in the light of the monetary and political history of both the period in which it *appears* to have been deposited and that which follows the ostensible date of deposit, since the reason for a hoard's existence may lie in an event which postdates the coins of which it is composed. Thus in periods of financial stress hoards will reflect the best material available to the hoarder, and such coinage must inevitably predate the coins of the currency crisis against which the hoarder is reacting.

Further complications arise from the life of individual coins and denominations at various periods. Gold of the early Empire had a long circulation life and in hoards where *aurei* occur with other denominations the gold coinage predates the silver. The South Shields hoard, for instance, contains *aurei* from Nero to Antoninus Pius and *denarii* from the Republic to Commodus. *Aes* coinage of the second century was recycled in the third century; with the attempt by Postumus to restore the fractional currency, large numbers of first- and second-century *sestertii* were restruck as double *sestertii,* sometimes unofficially. Hoards of early coins accumulated for restriking in the 260s are known. *Sestertius* hoards terminating with Antonine issues may be suspected of dating from the mid third century rather than from the late second century.

The distribution of hoards in Britain is largely determined by two factors. An absence or relatively lighter occurrence in the northern and Welsh military areas may be ascribed to a lower density of population and to the greater availability of safe storage facilities in forts than on civil sites. The latter consideration is emphasised by the observation that hoards on the frontier line tend to come from *vici*, the port settlement at South Shields, or from the urban site of Corbridge. The second important consideration is the agency by which hoards have been recovered. Until very recently the overwhelming proportion of hoards have been discovered in the course of ploughing. It follows that the majority of hoards will be from the modern arable areas of England and Wales (figs. 10-12).

Hoards from Roman urban contexts where these coincide with modern cities tend to be less well represented. It is impossible to determine whether or not this is due to factors in antiquity or unrecorded recovery over the centuries, but the reasonably high frequency of hoards at 'undisturbed' sites such as Caerwent, Verulamium and Silchester suggests that unrecorded recovery has distorted the picture.

Any systematic analysis of the hoards from Britain, of which some fifteen hundred are recorded, indicates that there are deposits representing all periods, thus emphasising the naturalness of hoarding in a society without banks, cheque books and all the paraphernalia of modern domestic finances (fig. 9). On the other hand, there are periods at which hoards are more heavily represented. Notably well attested are hoards closing with issues of Marcus Aurelius (161-80), Tetricus (270-3), Constantine (305-37) and Honorius (389-*c* 411). These peaks apart, there are substantial deposits in the first half of the third century and at the end of that century. Generalisation about the underlying causes of this pattern must vary from period to period but at only one period (Honorius-Constantine III) is it likely that an external military threat was an important factor in provoking the hoarding.

The correlation between hoards and major changes in the currency system is very strong. The peak achieved by hoards terminating with coins of Marcus Aurelius (fig. 10) can be explained by the abrupt decline in the silver content of the *denarius*, which began in the reign of Marcus and which accelerated under subsequent rulers (fig. 2). There can be little doubt that *denarii* from the reign of Marcus onwards were overvalued in relation to their metallic content, and earlier coins appear to have achieved premium status. A constant series of withdrawals from circulation of silver coinage characterises hoards of the first half of the third century, with each decline in the silver content of the coinage provoking the hoarding of the better coinage of the previous generation. 'Better' in

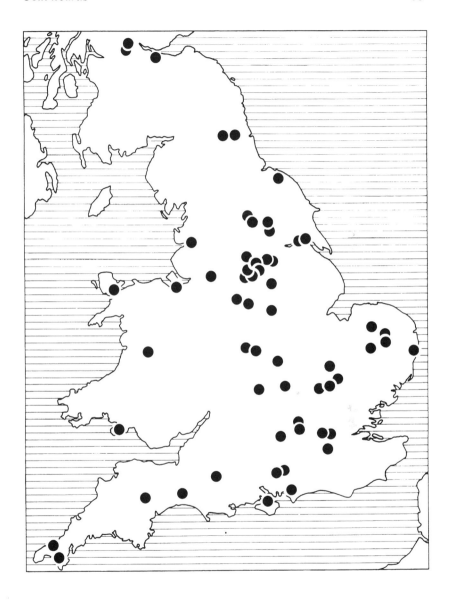

Fig. 10. Coin hoards, *c* 140-70 (after Robertson, 1974).

this context is a relative term since these coins will have been the base issues of the previous step in the decline of the currency. The last stage of this series of hoards coincides with the early years of the sole reign of Gallienus (258-68). The effects of the progressive withdrawal of better coins can be seen in the Dorchester hoard, of more than twenty thousand *denarii* and *antoniniani*.

Dorchester, Dorset   (*Numismatic Chronicle*, 5th series, 1939, 21-62)

Date	193-217	217-18	218-22	222-35	235-8	238-44
Number	26	1	127	6	74	8892
Percentage	0.12	0.005	0.6	0.3	0.36	43.0

Date	244-9	249-51	251-3	253	253-60
Number	6990	2331	1401	52	858
Percentage	32.2	11.2	6.7	0.25	4.10

Clearly the Dorchester hoard was assembled in the face of the abrupt decline in the fineness of the *antoninianus* in the sole reign of Gallienus. The scarcity of coinage predating Gordian III (238-44), when the silver coinage took one of its larger downward lurches, is eloquent testimony to the success of the state, and the individual, in removing coinage of higher metallic value from circulation.

The next generation of hoards was based on the 'better' earlier coinage of Valerian, Gallienus and Postumus, the Gallic usurper.

Piercebridge, Co. Durham   (*Coin Hoards* vol. 3, 1977, 72 ff)

Date	193-217	217-18	218-22	222-35	235-8	238-44
Number	—	—	—	—	1	—
Percentage	—	—	—	—	0.78	—

Date	244-9	249-51	251-3	253	253-60	260-2
Number	1	4	2	1	115	4
Percentage	0.78	3.12	1.56	0.78	90.0	3.20

A peak of hoards is achieved in the period covered by the decade of the Gallic Empire. Such hoards, consisting of base *antoniniani* of Victonius and Tetricus, frequently include both genuine coins together with radiate copies. In monetary terms these hoards are usually very poor, though a recent find of fifty-six thousand coins is an exception. The devaluation of the currency of the Gallic Empire by the Aurelianic reform, reinforced by measures of Probus (276-82), perhaps led to the abandonment of these hoards, the new coinage rendering them not worth the trouble of recovery

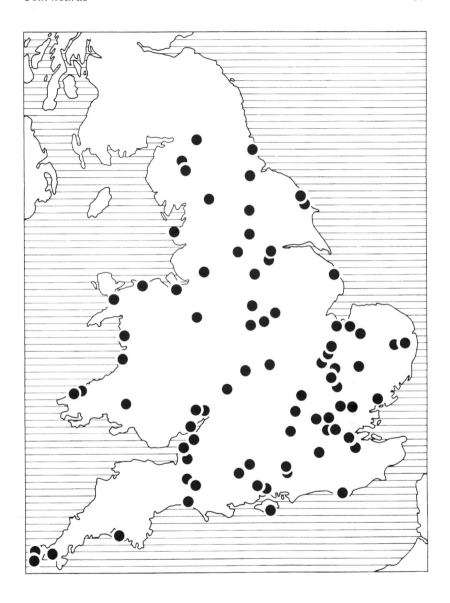

Fig. 11. Coin hoards, *c* 258-73 (after Robertson, 1974).

(fig. 11). This attitude to low-value coins would also explain the high incidence of Aurelianic hoards, which earn this classification only by virtue of the few reformed coins which comprise their terminal issues, the bulk of these hoards consisting of issues of the Gallic emperors. In any event, the prolific coinage of Carausius (286-93) swiftly replaced the Gallic Empire's issues and made good any shortage of Aurelianic coins. Carausian hoards are themselves prolific and reflect the demonetisation of the coinage of the usurper and his successor, Allectus, by the administration of Diocletian and Maximian after the recovery of Britain in 296.

The steady erosion in the weight of the *'follis'* after 305 led to withdrawals of early Diocletianic issues in several hoard-documented stages. A crucial point in this process appears to have occurred in the reign of Constantine in *c* 318 (by which time the *'follis'* had been reduced in weight from about 10 grams to about 3.5 grams). Coin hoards of the later years of the reign of Constantine are generally composed of issues immediately predating the reduction of the *centenionalis* to its weight of 2.5 grams in 330. The frequency of Constantinian hoards in general reflects the abundance of coinage in this period, whilst the peak for the period from Constantius II to Julian consists largely of hoards of demonetised issues of Magnentius or of copies of the *Fel Temp Reparatio* series.

A phenomenon of particular interest is the growth of silver hoarding from the middle of the fourth century. To a very great extent this must reflect the relative abundance of silver issues available from the middle of the reign of Constantius II (337-61) and especially in the reign of Valentinian and Valens (364-75).

Springhead, Kent   (*Numismatic Chronicle*, 7th series, 1965)

Date	*c* 356-60	361-4	364-78	378-83	383-8	388-92
Number	20	22	287	79	37	2
Percentage	4.47	4.92	64.20	17.67	8.27	0.44

The noticeably heavy incidence of such hoards in Britain has attracted attention. Britain had long served as a source of argentiferous lead for the Empire but the coinage comprising the hoards derives from continental mints. It has been suggested that the coinage reached Britain as payment to the lessees of the lead workings for their product, the silver for the coinage being extracted from the lead by the state, which bought the

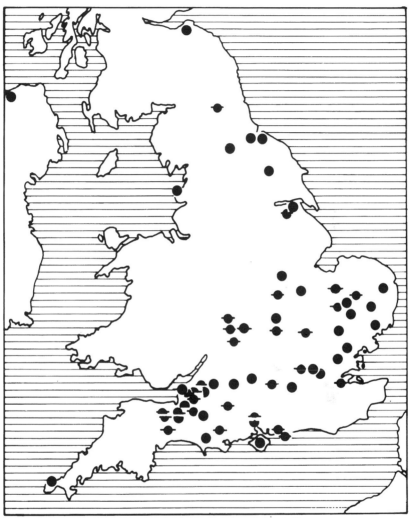

Fig. 12. Gold and silver hoards, 300-410 (after Archer, 1979).
(Barred circles are pre-400 hoards, plain circles hoards deposited after 400.)

heavier metal with the more precious. Some credibility is lent to this
suggestion by the incidence of silver hoards in the general area of the
Mendip lead deposits in Somerset and such devious financial dealing
would be well within the competence of the Roman financial administration of the fourth century.

There is a natural tendency to seek in gold and silver hoards of the later fourth century evidence for the impending collapse of the Roman administration of Britain, a collapse precipitated by events abroad but signalled by an apparent failure to prevent seaborne raiders attacking the island at will (fig. 12). Clearly such attacks will have produced a response in hoards although there is no especially significant evidence for hoarding at the time of the great invasion by a combination of barbarian enemies in 367.

Few hoards of the later fourth century consist of very large sums of money, though a hoard of six hundred *solidi* was found at Eye in Suffolk and between four hundred and fifty and six hundred *solidi* and about three thousand *siliquae* at Cleeve Prior in Worcestershire. A hoard of *solidi* from Corbridge, terminating with issues of Magnus Maximus, contained forty-eight coins, and in general hoards, whether of silver or a mixture of silver and gold, are of relatively modest proportions. A hoard from Hoxne, Suffolk, represents a variation of the purely monetary hoard of this period by including items of jewellery and silverware. This, the largest late Roman hoard recorded from Britain, comprises 563 *solidi* and almost 14,000 silver coins of various denominations. In bullion value the entire hoard would have been the equivalent of about 1,700 *solidi*. It would appear, in general, that those with large sums of money to protect sought other means than hoarding and that panic-stricken hoarding does not characterise the last years of Roman Britain despite the enigmatic entry in the Anglo-Saxon Chronicle under the year 418: 'In this year the Romans collected all the treasures which were in Britain, and hid some of them in the earth so that no one afterwards could find them, and some they took with them into Gaul.'

One class of hoard of the latest years of Roman Britain appears not within the area of Roman administration but peripheral to it. Hoards comprising a mixture of coins and fragments of chopped-up silver vessels have been found in Ireland and in Scotland. The source of the components of these hoards was clearly Britain but uncertainty remains as to whether they represent loot acquired by Irish or Pictish raiders, which was roughly hacked up in a division of spoils, or subsidies paid by a hard-pressed Roman administration to allies who could intervene to prevent raiding.

3
Museums

A number of museums house major collections of Roman coins, either of a general nature or from local sites. Students may, normally, obtain access to these collections by arrangement with the relevant department of the museum. Museums that display a wide range of coins in their public galleries include:

Ashmolean Museum of Art and Archaeology (Heberden Coin Room), Beaumont Street, Oxford OX1 2PH. Telephone: 01865 278000. Website: www.ashmol.ox.ac.uk

British Museum, Department of Coins and Medals, Great Russell Street, London WC1B. Telephone: 0207 323 8607. Website: www.britishmuseum.org

Castle Museum, Castle Park, Colchester, Essex CO1 1TJ. Telephone: 01206 282939.

Museum of London, London Wall, London EC2Y 5HN. Telephone: 020 7600 3699. Website: www.museum-london.org.uk

Museum of Scotland, Chambers Street, Edinburgh EH1 1JF. Telephone: 0131 247 4422. Website: www.nms.ac.uk

National Museum of Wales, Cathays Park, Cardiff CF10 3NP. Telephone: 029 2039 7951. Website: www.nmgw.ac.uk

A national identification and recording scheme for coins and antiquities found by metal detectorists and other field workers is available. The Museums, Libraries and Archives Portable Antiquities Scheme has established some fifty posts in museums and archaeological units throughout England and Wales. A list of local finds liaison officers can be obtained from:-

Portable Antiquities Scheme, British Museum, London WC1B 3DG.

4
Further reading

Background history
Frere, S. S. *Britannia: A History of Roman Britain.* Third edition, 1978.
Mattingly, D. *An imperial possession: Britain in the Roman empire.* 2006.
Salway, P. *Roman Britain.* 1981.

Catalogues
Carson, R. A. G., Hill, P. V., and Kent, J. P. C. *Late Roman Bronze Coinage.* 1960. (Cited as LRBC 1/2.)
Mattingly, H., and others. *Coins of the Roman Empire in the British Museum*, volumes 1-6. 1965-8.
Mattingly, H., and Sydenham, E. A. *The Roman Imperial Coinage*, volumes 1-10. 1923-94. (Cited as RIC.)

General works
Burnett, A. *Coinage in the Roman World.* 1987.
Casey, P. J., and Reece, R. (editors). *Coins and the Archaeologist.* Second edition, 1988.
Kent, J. P. C. *Roman Coins.* 1987.
Robertson, A. *An inventory of Roman-British coin hoards.* 2000.
Sutherland, H. *Roman Coins.* 1974.

Site reports
Allason-Jones, L., and McKay, B. *Coventina's Well: A shrine on Hadrian's Wall.* 1985.
Besley, E. *The Cunetio treasure: Roman coinage in the 3rd century AD.* 1983.
Casey, P. J., and Davies, J. L. *Excavations at Segontium.* (Carnarfon.)
Cunnliff, B. *Richborough.V.* 1968.

Index